50+ Super-Fun Math Activities 2

SCHOLASTIC

by Margaret Creed

NEW YORK • TORONTO • LONDON • AUCKLAND • SYDNEY
MEXICO CITY • NEW DELHI • HONG KONG • BUENOS AIRES

Teaching Resources

Edited by Jean Liccione

Cover design by Ka-Yeon Kim-Li

Interior design by Ellen Matlach Hassell for Boultinghouse & Boultinghouse, Inc.

Interior illustrations by Maxie Chambliss and Manuel Rivera

ISBN-13: 0-978-0-545-20817-8

ISBN-10: 0-545-20817-3

Printed in the U.S.A.

1 2 3 4 5 6 7 8 9 10   40   17 16 15 14 13 12 11 10

Contents

(continued on the next page)

✳ These activities include reproducibles.

✳ These activities include reproducibles.

Introduction

Welcome to *50+ Super-Fun Math Activities: Grade 2.* This book contains a unique collection of activities that reinforce important first-grade-level mathematics concepts and skills and support the math standards recommended by the National Council of Teachers of Mathematics (NCTM). See page 6, for more.

The book is organized by nine major content topics. When you're teaching a particular math concept or skill, just check the Contents page. Browse the activities listed under each topic to find just the right one to reinforce students' learning. Each major topic has projects, games, activities, and ready-to-use reproducibles designed to reinforce specific learning objectives. The activities will also get students interested and excited, and encourage them to value math and become confident mathematicians.

ACTIVITY FEATURES

The activities include grouping suggestions, lists of needed materials, teaching tips, step-by-step directions, and easy Assessment ideas. Some activities also include the following features:

◆ Extensions and Variations—ideas for taking the math skills and concepts further

◆ Home Links—quick and easy activities students can do at home with their families

◆ Writing Connections—suggestions for encouraging students to communicate and reinforce what they've learned through writing.

ABOUT GROUPING

Sometimes it's important for students to work together in groups or pairs, to collaborate and communicate. Sometimes they need to work independently. The activities in this book support a variety of needs, from independent to whole class work. You'll find a grouping suggestion at the beginning of each activity.

ASSESSING STUDENTS' WORK

NCTM recommends a variety of approaches to assessment of the various dimensions of a student's mathematical learning. The following assessment suggestions are incorporated throughout this book:

◆ ideas for group and class discussion

◆ ideas for journal writing and written response

◆ ideas for ongoing informal teacher observations

On pages 61–63, you'll also find suggested ways of observing and keeping records of students' work as well as a reproducible student Self-Evaluation Form and an Assessment Checklist and Scoring Rubric.

Remember that you can review students' self-assessments and their journals and written responses to see not only how well they understand concepts but also how well they express their mathematical understandings.

CONNECTIONS TO THE MATH STANDARDS

The activities in this book are designed to support you in meeting the following process standards for students in grades PreK–2 recommended by the National Council of Teachers of Mathematics (NCTM):

Problem Solving The activities promote a problem-solving approach to learning. Throughout the book, you'll find suggestions for encouraging students to develop, apply, and explain their problem-solving strategies.

Reasoning & Proof Suggestions in the last step of each activity can serve as prompts to help students draw logical conclusions, explain and justify their thinking, and "pull it together" to make sense of the mathematics skills and concepts they've just used. Activities encourage students to use patterns and relationships as they work.

Communication Activities include ideas for helping students organize and consolidate their mathematical thinking through class discussions and writing connections.

Connections Activities tie to the real world, to the interests of second-grade students, and to other areas of the curriculum. The purpose of many activities is to bridge conceptual and procedural knowledge, and to bridge different topics in mathematics.

Representation Students use manipulatives, pictures and diagrams, and numerical representations to complete the activities.

The grids below show how the activities correlate to the other math standards for grades PreK–2.

PAGE	Number & Operations	Algebra	Geometry	Measurement	Data Analysis & Probability
9	◆				
10	◆				◆
11					
13	◆				
14	◆				
15	◆				
16	◆				
17	◆				
18	◆				
20	◆				
22	◆				
23	◆				
25		◆			
26		◆			

PAGE	Number & Operations	Algebra	Geometry	Measurement	Data Analysis & Probability
28	◆	◆			
30			◆		◆
32			◆		
33			◆		
35	◆	◆			◆
36	◆		◆	◆	◆
37				◆	
39				◆	
40				◆	
42	◆				
44	◆				
46	◆				
47				◆	◆
48				◆	◆

PAGE	Number & Operations	Algebra	Geometry	Measurement	Data Analysis & Probability
50	◆			◆	
51	◆			◆	◆
52	◆		◆		
53	◆				
55	◆				
56	◆				
57	◆				
59	◆	◆			◆
60	◆	◆	◆		◆

Source: National Council of Teachers of Mathematics. (2000). *Principles and standards for school mathematics.* Reston: VA: NCTM. www.nctm.org

Any Time Is Math Time

Use these quick activities to keep children's minds on math at the beginning or end of class time, as they are lining up to change classes, or any time you have a few minutes to fill.

1. FOLLOW THE RHYTHM LEADER

Great for transition times, the first child who is ready begins a quiet tapping pattern. As other children finish their work and are ready, they copy the first child's pattern.

2. TODAY'S DATE

Especially later in the year, this is a great way to begin each day. As children file into the room, have them each write a number sentence for the day's date. Encourage them to be creative and to make their number sentences different from everyone else's. When everyone is done, check the equations as a class to be sure they equal the day's date.

3. LUNCH MATH

Whether lunches are ordered daily or weekly in your school, once you know how many children have ordered lunch on a particular day and how many have brought lunch, you can pose problems like the following:

◆ Three more people have brought their lunches than have ordered them. Fifteen have brought lunch. How many have ordered lunch?

◆ Two children are absent. How many children will be eating lunch today?
◆ Twenty children ordered pizza today. How many children brought lunch?

4. I'M THINKING OF A NUMBER

Play this guessing game with children. Pick a number and give clues about it, getting more and more specific as you need to. Ask children to raise their hands, but not say anything, when they think they know the number. For example: I'm thinking of a number between 12 and 30. The number has two 10s. It's an even number. When most or all children have raised their hands, have everyone call out the number. When children know how the game is played, they can choose the number and give clues.

5. DOUBLE TIME

At the end of the day or before beginning new activities, encourage children to look for doubles. For example, they could hold up both hands and say, 5 fingers and 5 fingers, or they could point out 2 boys and 2 girls. Besides their own bodies, they can look for doubles by counting the number of books on a shelf, and so on.

Any Time Is Math Time

More quick activities to keep children's minds on math...

6. FREEZE FRAME

One child watches the second hand of a clock while everyone else freezes in place for thirty seconds, forty seconds, one minute, and so on. Children will feel for themselves how long a minute can seem sometimes.

7. HOW MANY ARE HERE?

As children come into the classroom at the beginning of the day, choose a checker to help you keep track of how many are in the room already and how many more are due to arrive. If children sign or check an attendance sheet in the morning, you can ask volunteers to count how many have checked in and then ask the rest of the children to figure out how many more children are expected. As groups of children enter the room, a child can keep a running tally of how many have arrived.

8. SKIP-COUNT OFF!

As children stand in line, they can count by 1s, 2s, 3s, 4s or 5s. As children count off, they will have to figure out who should say the next number in the sequence.

9. CLASSIFICATION LINEUP

Before children get in line at different times during the day, you might want to have them sort themselves into groups. For example, they could form groups according to what color shirts or pants they are wearing, what month their birthdays fall, what they ate for breakfast, and so on. You could also have them line up shortest to tallest or tallest to shortest.

10. FIND A NUMBER

While waiting for some children to finish activities or clean up work areas, challenge other children to find, for example, sets of 5, 12, or 17 of something in the room. Children don't have to leave their seats to find the objects. For example, children might say there are 12 windowpanes or paintings on the wall. They might say there are 5 tables or chairs. Challenge children to try and name items as close to the given number as possible.

Number Seesaw

On this interactive bulletin board, children move the seesaw up and down to compare numbers.

PREPARATION

Make two sets of cards with the numbers 0–9 on each set. Also make cards for greater than (>) and less than (<). Write the words for the symbols on the backs of the cards. Cut a triangle and a long, thin rectangle of oak tag to use as the seesaw. Attach the seesaw to the bulletin board so it moves. Set up the bulletin board with pockets for each set of cards, as shown.

DIRECTIONS

1. Talk with children about ways they can determine which of two numbers is greater. Children may suggest putting out counters, comparing the number of 10s and 1s, knowing which comes first in the counting sequence, or other ideas.

2. Introduce the seesaw bulletin board. Explain that if two numbers are equal, the seesaw should balance. If one number is greater than another, the number of greater value will make the seesaw go down on one end. Demonstrate by pinning two cards from one pocket at one end of the seesaw, making a 2-digit number. Then pin two cards from the other pocket at the other end of the seesaw, making another 2-digit number. Ask children which number is greater. How should the seesaw look?

3. Show children the symbol cards for greater than and less than and make sure they know what each sign means. Place the correct symbol between the two numbers. Then tilt the seesaw toward the greater number and record the comparison using a number sentence, for example: 35 > 20.

4. Encourage pairs of children to come to the board, construct 2-digit numbers, pin them on the seesaw, and decide which is greater. They should then place the correct symbol, tilt the seesaw, and record the comparison.

Grouping

Whole class

You'll Need

◆ Bulletin board
◆ Pushpins or thumbtacks
◆ Index cards
◆ Oak tag or other heavy paper
◆ Markers

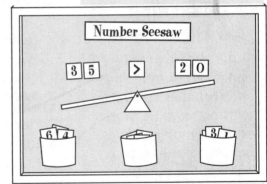

ASSESSMENT

Observe children to see what they know about relationships between numbers. Do they place the symbols > and < correctly?

Rolling for Numbers

Each roll of the number cube brings out another 2-digit number.

DIRECTIONS

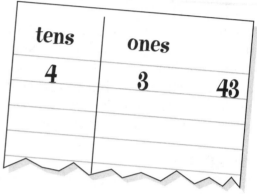

tens	ones	
4	3	43

1. Show children how to make a simple place-value recording sheet like the one shown.

2. Divide the class into groups of two and tell pairs that they will be rolling for numbers. The goal is to get the largest number on each roll. Each child in a pair rolls the number cube and records the number in either the tens or ones column. Children will have to be strategic about where they place the first number they roll. Partners can then take turns writing the number and saying, for example: Forty-three—four tens and three ones.

3. Have children alternate rolls until they have recorded several numbers.

4. After pairs have finished, have them circle the numbers that have a greater digit in the ones place than in the tens place. Discuss with children what the numbers would be if the greater digit were in the tens place.

✛✛✛ VARIATION

Partners can take turns rolling the number cube twice and recording a number without the other child seeing the results. Children can give clues for their partner to guess the number.

ASSESSMENT

Listening to children as they talk about tens and ones and 2-digit numbers will give you an idea of how familiar they are with the concept of place value. You might want to ask questions like the following to check children's understanding.

◆ Which is greater: a number with 4 tens, 5 tens, or 6 tens?

◆ Which number is greater: 7 tens and 8 ones, or 8 tens and 7 ones? How do you know?

Vacation Mix-Up

Children use logic to put the days in order in this mixed-up vacation story.

PREPARATION
You may want to write all the words for the ordinal numbers from *first* to *twentieth* on the chalkboard or chart paper for children to use as a reference.

DIRECTIONS
1. Tell children that Toby and her family went on a vacation. Toby wrote about each day in her journal, but the pages got mixed up. Explain that they will help Toby put her journal in order.

2. Read the following to tell children the first part of the story:

   On the first day we packed all our bags and got the supplies. On the second day we drove away from home. On the third day we finally stopped in the mountains. On the fourth day we climbed to the top of a mountain and took pictures of mountain goats. On the fifth day we headed to the lake.

   Explain that after that, the story gets mixed up. Tell children they'll help Toby put her story back in order.

3. Distribute reproducible page 12. Have children cut apart the sentences and look for clues to help them order the sentences correctly. When they have an order they like, they should paste the sentences on drawing paper in order. Then they write the correct ordinal numbers (beginning with *sixth*) to complete the sentences. Encourage children to draw pictures to illustrate the story.

4. Invite children to compare their stories with others in the class. Did everyone put the events in the same order? What clues helped?

➤➤➤ EXTENSION
Children might enjoy continuing the story by telling what happened from the fourteenth to twentieth days. Ask children to write sentences, draw pictures, and label using ordinal numbers.

 ASSESSMENT
Read children's stories to see whether they understand ordinal numbers and were able to add them to their stories. **Answers: A.** seventh **B.** ninth **C.** eleventh **D.** tenth **E.** sixth **F.** twelfth **G.** thirteenth, **H.** eighth.

 **Grouping**
Individual

 **You'll Need**

For each child:
◆ **Vacation Mix-Up (reproducible page 12)**
◆ Scissors
◆ Paste
◆ Pencil
◆ Drawing paper
◆ Crayons or markers

Vacation Mix-Up

Cut apart the sentences.
Look for clues to put the days in order.
Then glue the sentences to a separate
sheet of paper.
Write *sixth* through *thirteenth* to finish
each sentence.

On the _____ day we gathered wood for cooking
and hiked around the lake for the first time.   A

On the _____ day we ate soggy food
and hiked in the mud.   B

On the _____ day we hiked and then had
our last cookout for dinner.   C

On the _____ day the sun was back
and we went swimming.   D

On the _____ day we got to the lake
and set up our tents.   E

On the _____ day we packed up the car
and drove away from the lake.   F

On the _____ day we got home again.   G

On the _____ day it rained from morning till night.   H

50+ Super-Fun Math Activities: Grade 2 © 2010 by Scholastic Inc.

Stand and Be Counted

The whole class can stand and be counted as they join in this number-making activity.

PREPARATION

Label nine index cards *hundreds,* nine *tens,* and nine *ones.*

DIRECTIONS

1. Invite children to join you in creating numbers. Draw a place-value chart on the chalkboard and have children make charts of their own on scrap paper. Show children the cards and explain that for each turn you will be passing out some of the cards.

Hundreds	Tens	Ones

2. Shuffle the deck. Distribute part of it. Children who do not receive cards act as Counters. You may also want to appoint some children as Checkers in each round to make sure that numbers are counted and recorded correctly.

3. Children with hundreds cards come to the front of the room. The Counters count the number of children. Then a Counter records how many hundreds on the place-value chart. Next, children with cards for tens, and then ones, come forward to be counted. Have the Counters record the correct numbers in the tens and ones places on the chart.

4. For the next round, distribute a different number of cards. Make sure that every child participates in different roles.

5. When you have gone through a few rounds, begin mixing up the order in which you call children with cards to come forward.

▶▶▶ **EXTENSIONS**

◆ Record the numbers as children build them. In each round ask if the new number is greater than, less than, or equal to the number recorded in the last round.

◆ Add six more cards to the set of tens and ones you made. Use the cards when you're teaching regrouping. Show children how to regroup ones to make another 10, or tens to make another 100, when there are more than 9 in any place on the place-value chart.

Grouping

Whole class

You'll Need

◆ 27 small index cards

Teaching Tip

Children who need more work with place-value concepts can do the activity using only the tens and ones cards.

Number Scramble

Children scramble to compare and order numbers.

Grouping

Small group or whole class

You'll Need

◆ Small slips of paper or index cards

◆ Pencils

DIRECTIONS

1. Tell children they will be unscrambling numbers to put them in order from least (or smallest) to greatest (or largest).

2. Give each child a piece of paper. Ask everyone to think of a number less than 100 and write it on his or her slip of paper.

3. Have children form small groups and share their numbers. Group members figure out which number is the smallest and which is the largest, and order the numbers in the group from least to greatest.

4. When groups have ordered their numbers, bring the class together and check the numbers within each group. Then tell children to get ready for a BIG number scramble! Have children begin to order the numbers of all class members. Ask questions along the way, such as:

   ◆ Who thinks they wrote the smallest number of all? What number did you write?

   ◆ Did anyone write a smaller number than that?

   ◆ Who has an even number? an odd number?

   ◆ What is a number that is missing between these two numbers [give two]?

   Encourage children to suggest ways to make the ordering of so many numbers easier.

5. When everyone's number has been put in correct order, you might want to have children stand in order from the smallest to the greatest number and ask them to tell about their numbers in relation to the numbers on each side. For example: 24 is greater than 19 and less than 25.

 ASSESSMENT

Note how easily children are able to compare the numbers within a group. Listen to group members' reasons for ordering the numbers the way they did.

Set It Up

Children invent their own addition problems by categorizing sets of objects that they will add.

DIRECTIONS

1. Distribute the paper bags and ask each child to put some (4–15) objects from the room (pencils, crayons, paper clips, erasers, and so on) into their bags. Children make a list of the objects they put into the bags and put the list in the bags as well.

2. Gather all the bags and mix them up. Divide the class into pairs, give each child a bag, and ask pairs of children to empty the bags and decide how they can sort the objects into groups. For example, they might decide to put pencils and crayons together because you can write with them. They might put paper clips and scissors together because they are both silver. Children can sort the objects into as many groups as they like. Let them know they don't have to use all the objects in the bags.

3. Children work together to record addition sentences about the groups of objects they've made. The number of addends in each equation will depend on the number of sets of objects children created. Children use the lists to return the objects to the bags.

4. Pairs can exchange bags with another group and repeat the grouping and adding activity.

5. The number sentences children write in this activity will be interesting to discuss. For instance, children can share the different number combinations they've found that add up to the same sum.

ASSESSMENT

Check children's work by observing the strategies they use to add the sets of objects. Children who have to count every object in order to get to the total are at a different level from children who use other addition strategies, such as counting on or remembering facts.

Grouping

Pairs

You'll Need

◆ One small paper bag for each child

◆ Small, countable objects

Home Link

Encourage children to play a similar game with a family member. Each person collects a set of objects, sorts them, and then adds. Have children record their equations and bring them back to share with the class.

Stamp-It Addition

With their own stamps and some paper, children make art they can add!

DIRECTIONS

1. Provide each child with half of a cut potato. Have children draw, or mark in some way, a simple design on the potato. Then visit each child and cut out the design with a sharp knife.

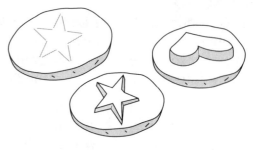

2. Show children how to dip the potato into paint and press it on paper to make an image. Then provide each child with a shallow dish of paint or a stamp pad.

3. Have children fold a piece of drawing paper in half and then draw a line on the fold. Then have them fill their papers with stamps. They may also want to trade stamps with a classmate to make a second group of designs.

4. When children have finished stamping, have them use a separate sheet of paper to write addition sentences about their stamped papers. For example, they can add the number of stamps they made on the top and bottom of the paper to find the total. They could also circle two groups of stamps and write addition sentences. Challenge children to write as many addition sentences about their papers as possible.

5. Have children share their work with classmates.

ASSESSMENT

Review children's papers and addition sentences. Note how accurately they counted and added the groups.

To 100

Players add until they reach 100.

PREPARATION
For each group, make number cards for 1 to 38. You might give children practice in writing numbers and counting by having each group write the numbers to make their own set of cards.

DIRECTIONS
1. Divide the class into small groups and distribute sets of number cards. Explain the addition card game. Children will pick cards until they get to 100 or more—the trick is knowing when they get there!

2. To start, each player picks a card. The player with the lowest number goes first. That player gathers all the cards, returns them to the pile, and shuffles the cards.

3. Players take turns drawing cards from the pile. They keep the cards they've picked until they estimate the sum of their numbers to be 100 or more. The player then calls out "100!" Other players do the calculation to check that the sum of the numbers on the cards is 100 or over 100. Counters, paper and pencil, or calculators can be used to find the total. If the total is not 100 or more, the player must put all of his or her cards back in the stack and start over picking cards.

4. Players drop out of the game when they have reached 100 or more. Play continues until everyone has reached 100 or until the cards are gone.

ASSESSMENT
Children might consider questions like the following as they assess their addition skills: Without doing the addition, how do you know when you're getting near 100? when you're over 100?

Grouping
Small groups

You'll Need

◆ Index cards
◆ Markers
◆ Calculators (optional)
◆ Counters (optional)

Tug-of-War Addition

Children use all their mental might to play this addition game!

Grouping

Pairs

You'll Need

For each pair:

◆ Tug-of-Addition (reproducible page 19)

◆ Number cube labeled 1–6

◆ 2 counters or other playing pieces

DIRECTIONS

1. Distribute reproducible page 19 and invite children to play this addition game. Players choose to help Team A or Team B in an addition tug. The point of the game is to "pull" one's playing piece off the board.

2. Players both put their playing pieces on Start. In the first move of the game, partners each roll the number cube and move that number of spaces in opposite directions from Start. They look at the numbers they each land on and estimate what the sum will be. Have players write their guesses. They then add the two numbers and compare the actual sums with their estimates. The child whose estimate is closer to the sum rolls the number cube first on the next turn. Both children must then move their pieces in that player's direction on the board.

3. Play continues until one player has moved off of the board, winning the tug addition.

ASSESSMENT

Talk with children about the strategies they use to estimate the sums. Ask them how they can they get better at estimating.

50+ Super-Fun Math Activities: Grade 2 © 2010 by Scholastic Inc.

Name _____

Tug-of-War Addition

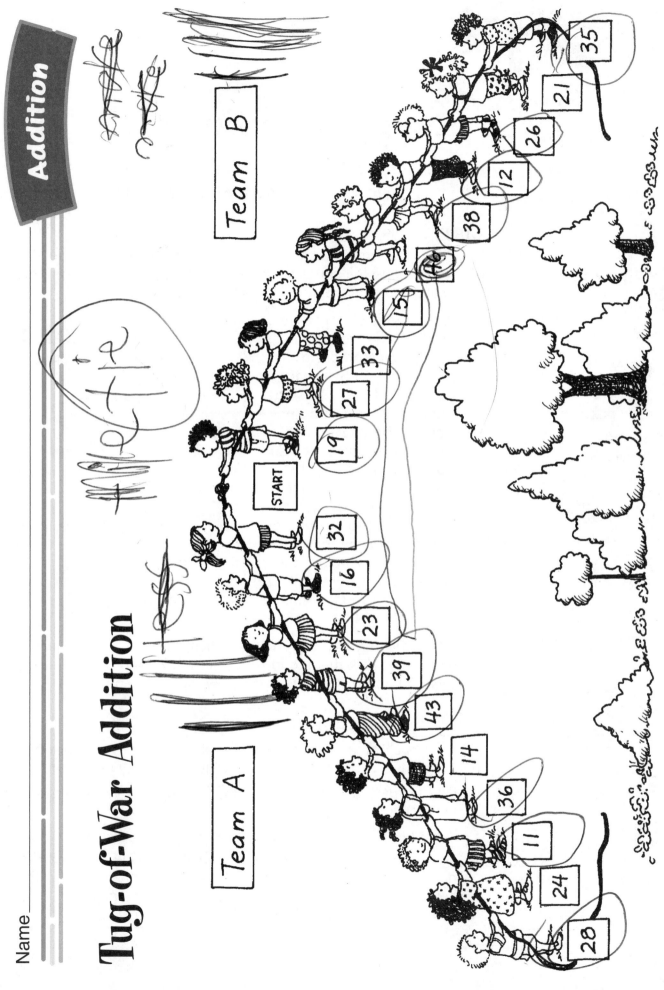

Team A

Team B

START

Step-Down Subtraction

Children will "step right down" as they subtract their way to the bottom of the staircase.

Grouping

Pairs

You'll Need

For each pair:

◆ **Step Down Subtraction (reproducible page 21)**

◆ Number cube labeled 1–6

◆ Pencils

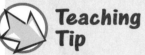

Teaching Tip

Some children might benefit from numbering each step on the way down before they begin the game. This may help them see the relationship between the numbers they are subtracting and the idea of counting back by that number.

DIRECTIONS

1. Invite children to imagine they have been to the top of the Empire State Building and are on their way back down the steps. Finally, they have only 25 steps left to go!

2. Divide the class in pairs and distribute the Step Down Subtraction reproducible. Explain that partners each start at the top of the steps. One should be X and the other O. They take turns rolling the number cube and moving down from 1 to 6 steps. On the step where they land, they should draw an X or an O to record their own move. Then they write a subtraction sentence for the move, beginning with 25 and taking away the number of their first roll.

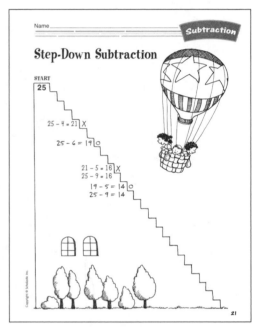

3. When children are finished, invite them to share the sentences they wrote. Ask them to look back at the Xs and Os. Did they ever end up on the same step? How did that happen?

ASSESSMENT

As children work, notice what strategies they use to subtract. Listen as partners talk about the numbers they use.

◆ Do they use the steps on the sheet to count back from a number?

◆ What patterns do they notice in the equations they write?

◆ How do they do the computation when subtracting from 2-digit numbers? Is their subtraction an "automatic" process when they get to basic facts, or do they use a counting technique to determine the answers?

Step-Down Subtraction

goal count down to

START

25

24 23 22 21 20 19 18 17 16 15 14 13 12 11 10 9 8 7 6 5 4 3 2 1 0

goal made

21

Take-Away Patterns

Children discover patterns in a string of subtraction sentences.

Grouping

Whole class

You'll Need

◆ Paper
◆ Pencils

Writing Connection

Have children write one or two sentences to tell what happens when they write every possible subtraction sentence for a number.

DIRECTIONS

1. Discuss with children what they know about subtracting numbers. Make a list of their responses on the chalkboard or chart paper.

2. Invite children to pick a number between 9 and 21 and write every subtraction sentence available for that number, beginning by subtracting zero and ending by subtracting the number from itself. Encourage children to write the subtraction sentences neatly one beneath the other. This will help them find patterns when they look at their completed lists.

11 − 0 = 11
11 − 1 = 10
11 − 2 = 9
11 − 3 = 8
11 − 4 = 7
11 − 5 = 6
11 − 6 = 5
11 − 7 = 4
11 − 8 = 3
11 − 9 = 2
11 − 10 = 1
11 − 11 = 0

3. After children have their lists of subtraction sentences, ask them to share them with the class. Encourage the class to identify patterns they notice in the lists. Prompt them with questions such as these:

◆ Find where the number pattern reverses itself. *(halfway through)*

◆ What happens when you subtract an even number from an odd number? *(You get an odd number.)*

◆ What about when you subtract an even number from an even number? *(You get an even number.)*

◆ What happens when you subtract an odd number from an odd number? *(You get an even number.)*

◆ How did you know when you had written all the possible subtraction sentences?

Subtraction Action

Children get in on the action as they regroup to subtract.

PREPARATION
Create number cards for the numbers 10 through 49 for each pair.

DIRECTIONS

1. Write these two subtraction problems on the chalkboard:

$$\begin{array}{r} 23 \\ -18 \\ \hline \end{array} \qquad \begin{array}{r} 48 \\ -15 \\ \hline \end{array}$$

   Ask children if they can tell, just by looking at the problems whether they'll have to regroup to subtract. Gather ideas from several children.

2. Divide the class into pairs and give each pair a set of the number cards, a copy of reproducible page 24, and the connecting cubes.

3. Tell children to shuffle the cards and each pick one. They each write the numbers they've picked in the first column on their recording sheet. Then they use the cubes to model the higher number by connecting sets of tens and leaving the ones separate.

4. Have children look at the lower number and predict whether they need to regroup to subtract it from the number they modeled with cubes. Remind them to look at the number in the ones place. Encourage children to record their prediction in the second column.

5. Children can now subtract the lower number from the higher number, using the cubes to check whether their prediction about regrouping was correct. They record the results in the third column. Finally, have children write a subtraction sentence that shows what they did. They can continue picking cards, estimating, and checking until the cards have all been picked.

6. Talk with children about the activity. Were they able to predict when they would need to regroup? How did they know? Did they get better at predicting?

ASSESSMENT
Ask children what they learned about subtracting tens and ones. Note whether they are able to make generalizations about when it is necessary to regroup and when it is not.

Grouping
Pairs

You'll Need

For each pair:

◆ **Subtraction Action (reproducible page 24)**

◆ 50 connecting cubes (or other countable objects)

◆ Paper

◆ Pencils

◆ Index cards

Teaching Tip

You might suggest that children place the card with the higher number above the one with the lower number, so that they can more easily compare how many ones the numbers have.

Subtraction Action

CARDS PICKED	NEED TO REGROUP?	PREDICTION CORRECT?	SUBTRACTION SENTENCE
	Yes No	Yes No	
	Yes No	Yes No	
	Yes No	Yes No	
	Yes No	Yes No	
	Yes No	Yes No	
	Yes No	Yes No	
	Yes No	Yes No	
	Yes No	Yes No	
	Yes No	Yes No	

Tap, Tap, Clap

Children will really feel the beat as they work with these patterns!

DIRECTIONS

1. Tell children that they will be working with sounds and rhythms. If rhythm instruments are available, distribute them to children.

2. Have children listen carefully as you create a simple pattern using an instrument or by clapping and tapping your lap or a tabletop. For example: tap, clap, tap, clap; or tap, tap, clap, tap, tap, clap. Pause before you repeat the same rhythmic pattern, but repeat each pattern several times until children can pick it up and follow along. When most children have figured out the pattern and are able to follow it, stop and let them continue it on their own.

3. Repeat the process for more patterns, making each pattern slightly more complicated than the last. Invite children to make up some rhythm patterns of their own for the class to follow.

4. Then play a piece of music, or have the class sing a familiar song, and challenge children to tap out the rhythm.

 ASSESSMENT

Notice how quickly children are able to join in and continue the patterns.

EXTENSIONS

◆ Assign a number or letter to each element of a sound pattern. Have children translate the taps and claps into numbers or letters. For example, tap, tap, clap could become 1, 1, 2 or A, A, B.

◆ Read some poems and have children chant along. What patterns can children find in the rhyming words of a poem? Here are two examples:

> A drippy sky, a rainy day.
> I wish we could go out to play.
> Oh, look now, here's the sun.
> Come on out and have some fun.

> There are two things I can't get right,
> No matter how I've tried:
> I wind the cat up every night
> And put the clock outside.

 **Grouping**

Whole class

 You'll Need

◆ Rhythm instruments (optional)

◆ Recordings of different sorts of music with strong rhythms (optional)

 **Home Link**

Invite children to share the activity with family members by making up and tapping out different rhythms. Encourage children also to use step and voice rhythms.

Now You See It

Once they see them, children will have fun extending these visual patterns.

Grouping

Small groups

You'll Need

For each child:

◆ **Now You See It (reproducible page 27)**

◆ Crayons or markers

Writing Connection

Encourage children to answer the following question: What would you tell a friend who asked, "What's a pattern"?

DIRECTIONS

1. Using objects in the classroom or an arrangement of children in the front of the room, create patterns. Ask children to identify the patterns they see. You might ask children to stand boy-girl-boy-girl, or sneakers-shoes-sneakers-shoes.

2. Discuss patterns that children can see around them. For example, your classroom might have a checkered floor, or a child might be wearing a striped shirt. Encourage children to be creative as they think of patterns like these to add to the discussion.

3. As children find patterns, encourage them to think about how the patterns are different. In the above examples, a checkered floor has two parts that repeat over and over; it's an A-B or a 1-2 pattern. A striped shirt might be four colors alternating in narrower and wider stripes. Ask children how they would name such a pattern.

4. Divide the class into groups and give each child reproducible page 27. Have them look at the patterns at the top of the page and continue them. Encourage children to talk about the patterns as they work.

5. The rest of the page gives children the chance to create their own patterns. Allow time for children to share their patterns with their groups and to talk about all the different patterns they made. Ask children to identify the elements that made each pattern. Was the pattern created by repeating shapes, repeating colors, repeating positions of an object, or other?

ASSESSMENT

Use these questions to help children evaluate what they know about creating patterns:

◆ Did I repeat the parts of my pattern exactly the same way each time?

◆ Did I repeat enough of a pattern that others could continue it?

Now You See It

Look at each pattern. Then continue the pattern.

1.

2.

3.

Now make your own patterns. Show them to a friend.

4.

5.

6.

What's Next?

Children find out what's next as they continue these number patterns.

Grouping

Small groups

You'll Need

For each child:

◆ What's Next? (reproducible page 29)

◆ Small counters, such as beans, that will fit squares of reproducible page 29

Writing Connection

Suggest that children reproduce their favorite number pattern and then write a sentence that describes the pattern.

DIRECTIONS

1. Distribute reproducible page 29 and ask children what patterns they can find. For example, point out that each number in a row is 1 more than the one before it. Ask questions like the following about other patterns children can look for:

   ◆ What do you notice about each column going down the chart?

   ◆ What do you notice about diagonal rows?

   ◆ What other patterns do you see in the chart?

2. Distribute counters. Also provide each group with a few of the following number patterns.

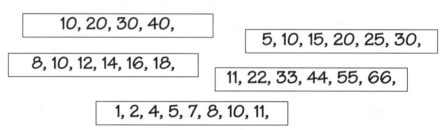

| 10, 20, 30, 40, |
| 8, 10, 12, 14, 16, 18, |
| 5, 10, 15, 20, 25, 30, |
| 11, 22, 33, 44, 55, 66, |
| 1, 2, 4, 5, 7, 8, 10, 11, |

   Have groups figure out the patterns and write the next five numbers in the sequence. They can use the manipulatives as markers on the hundred frame. The markers provide a good visual reinforcement of the pattern, and the hundred frame will help children find the next numbers in the sequence.

3. Invite groups to make up their own number patterns. Encourage them to show a pattern they've started to another group. Can others continue their patterns?

ASSESSMENT

Talk with groups about what they're doing to figure out each pattern. Encourage them to try different ideas until they find one that works.

What's Next?

1	2	3	4	5	6	7	8	9	10
11	12	13	14	15	16	17	18	19	20
21	22	23	24	25	26	27	28	29	30
31	32	33	34	35	36	37	38	39	40
41	42	43	44	45	46	47	48	49	50
51	52	53	54	55	56	57	58	59	60
61	62	63	64	65	66	67	68	69	70
71	72	73	74	75	76	77	78	79	80
81	82	83	84	85	86	87	88	89	90
91	92	93	94	95	96	97	98	99	100

Lines, Curves, and Corners

What's around the corner? Children find out as they analyze real-world objects around them.

Grouping

Small groups

You'll Need

For each child:

◆ Lines, Curves, and Corners (reproducible page 31)

◆ Pencil

Home Link

Encourage children to bring their recording sheets home with them and to look for more objects with the characteristics on the list in their neighborhoods and homes. Add this new information to the class graph.

DIRECTIONS

1. Review with children what they know about 2- and 3-dimensional shapes, as well as straight lines, curved lines, and corners.

2. Explain to children that they will be looking at the things around them to find objects that have lines, corners, or curves.

3. Distribute reproducible page 31 and go over the headings with children. Explain that small groups will take turns looking in the classroom or school playground for 3-dimensional objects and 2-dimensional shapes with the characteristics listed: "Shapes with Curves," "Shapes with Corners," and "Shapes with Straight Lines." They will use the reproducible page to record the name of each item with the characteristics that they see.

ASSESSMENT

Note how easily children identify aspects of an object's shape. Listen to group members as they talk about the characteristics of the objects.

▶▶▶ EXTENSION

When all the groups have collected information, work with the whole class to make a Venn diagram showing how many different objects with the listed characteristics children found. Overlaps of common characteristics can be shown in the center of the diagram.

Lines, Curves, and Corners

WHAT IT LOOKS LIKE	NAME OF OBJECT	FLAT	TAKES UP SPACE	NUMBER OF SIDES
Shapes with Curves	1.			
	2.			
	3.			
Shapes with Corners	1.			
	2.			
	3.			
Shapes with Straight Lines	1.			
	2.			
	3.			

50+ Super-Fun Math Activities: Grade 2 © 2010 by Scholastic Inc.

Mystery Shapes

As children follow directions, familiar shapes appear.

Grouping

Whole class

You'll Need

For each child:
◆ 2 sheets of dot paper
◆ Pencil

Writing Connection

Have children write how they can describe, in numbers, a shape they drew on dot paper. For example, a square might be 2-2-2-2.

DIRECTIONS

1. Distribute the dot paper. Explain that you are going to give directions for drawing a mystery shape. When you finish, children will hold up their shapes, compare them, and identify them. What mystery shapes will emerge? Are they all the same?

2. Give instructions such as these:

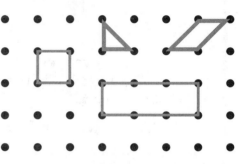

   ◆ Draw a shape that has 2 dots on each side. (*square, triangle, rhombus*)

   ◆ Draw a shape that has sides of 2 dots and 4 dots. (*rectangle*)

3. Call on volunteers to give instructions for drawing larger shapes. Point out that directions can vary depending on the number of dots on a side and whether the lines are drawn down, up, left, or right. The directions will also determine the size of the shape.

4. Challenge the class to develop easy-to-understand instructions for drawing other shapes.

ASSESSMENT

Observe how children follow directions for drawing the shapes to determine if they understand basic directions. Can they name the shapes?

➔➔➔ EXTENSION

Encourage children to create instructions for drawing other shapes such as a star, block letters, or shapes within shapes.

Where at the Fair?

Children spend a day at the fair as they use their map skills.

DIRECTIONS

1. Invite children to share experiences they have had at a fair. For children who haven't been to a state or county fair, explain that it is a place where people can play games, eat food, enjoy rides, and see farm animals and cooking and crafts exhibits.

2. Distribute reproducible page 34. Explain that the page shows a map of a fairgrounds. Talk about the things to see and do. Then tell children to put their pencils on the lower left square that says "County Fair." Have them draw a line 4 squares to the right and 4 squares up. Ask them where they are. Discuss any other straight-line route they might follow to get to the popcorn stand.

3. Have children draw items listed on the reproducible to finish the map.

4. Encourage children to think of directions for getting to different places in the fair, starting in the lower left-hand corner. For example: Go 2 squares up. Go 2 squares right.

5. Then have pairs take turns directing each other to different places on their maps. Children might use a different-color crayon to draw each route. To check directions, partners should say where they end up.

6. Invite children to describe what they saw at the fair and share what they drew.

ASSESSMENT

Check children's maps for placement of additional drawings. Talk about the maps and the paths children traced. Note whether they mention places along the routes they followed.

Grouping

Pairs

You'll Need

For each child:

◆ **Where at the Fair? (reproducible page 34)**

◆ Crayons or markers (different colors)

◆ Pencil

Writing Connection

Encourage children to choose their favorite place at the fair and write the directions to get there, starting in the lower left-hand corner. Then have them answer these questions: Where did you go at the fair? What did you see?

Name_____

Where at the Fair?

◆ **Draw a crafts tent.**

◆ **Draw a place for the cows.**

◆ **Draw one more thing you would like to see at the fair.**

50+ Super-Fun Math Activities: Grade 2 © 2010 by Scholastic Inc.

Problems and More

Here are some problems you can pose to children. On the next page is a reproducible with problems children can tackle on their own.

1. THE BIG SLEEP

José went to bed at 9 o'clock.
Jeremy went to bed at 8:30.

◆ Who went to bed first?

◆ How much earlier did he go to bed?

2. TUMMY MONEY

Bill and Jessica brought snack money to the park. Jessica had 1 quarter, 5 dimes, 3 nickels, and 2 pennies. Bill had 2 quarters, 2 dimes, 1 nickel, and 5 pennies.

◆ How much money does Bill have?

◆ How much money does Jessica have?

◆ Who has more money?

◆ How much money do they have altogether?

3. 36¢

How many different ways can you show 36¢ using pennies, nickels, dimes, or quarters?

4. CALENDAR MATH

Ask children to look at a calendar page for the current month.

◆ What is the date today?

◆ What date will it be 7 days from today?

◆ How many weeks are there until the end of the month? How many days?

◆ How many Saturdays are there in this month?

5. ALL THE WAY AROUND

Pick three things to measure. Find out how many inches they are all the way around. (Some ideas of things to measure: a poster, a desk- or tabletop, a book, a tile on the floor.)

◆ How can you find out how many inches around a ball is?

6. DO I HALF TO?

Tony's mother gave him 12 cookies. He gave half of his cookies to his friend Rodney. When Lucy came home, Tony and Rodney each gave Lucy 2 cookies.

◆ How many cookies did Tony give Rodney?

◆ How many cookies did Tony have left?

◆ How many cookies does each child have after Tony and Rodney give cookies to Lucy?

7. THREE-PACKS ON SALE!

Ms. Martinez bought 12 three-packs of juice. How many cans of juice does she have? Draw pictures, or use counters, if you need to.

Problems and More

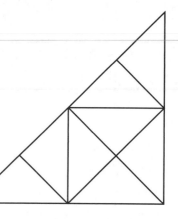

1. TRICKY TRIANGLES

How many triangles can you find
in this shape? Share ideas with
your classmates. Who found the
most triangles?

2. TIME AFTER TIME

How are the clocks the same?
How are they different?

_____

_____

3. HALF AGAIN

Draw the missing
half of each shape.

4. A CODE FOR YOU!

ABC	DEF	GHI	JKL	MNO	PQR	STU	VWX	YZ
1	2	3	4	5	6	7	8	9

Use the code. Write your name.
Add to find the value of all the letters in your name.

Name _____ Value _____

Find the value of some other words you know.

50+ Super-Fun Math Activities: Grade 2 © 2010 by Scholastic Inc.

Make a Schedule

Children see time in two different ways as they match clocks and complete a daily schedule.

DIRECTIONS

1. Use models to review telling time on both an analog and a digital clock. Discuss the different activities that children might do in the morning, afternoon, and night.

2. Distribute reproducible page 38 and point out the clockfaces. Explain to children that they will match clocks that show the same time. They should cut out the digital clocks from the bottom of the page and glue each one in place next to the analog clock that shows the same time.

3. After children match the clocks, it's time to make a daily schedule! Ask children to think of activities they do at the times shown. Then ask them to write what they do on the lines next to each clock.

ASSESSMENT

Ask children how they know the times on two clocks match.

Grouping

Individual

You'll Need

For each child:

◆ **Make a Schedule (reproducible page 38)**

◆ Scissors

◆ Glue or paste

◆ Pencil

Home Link

Encourage children to ask a family member to help them make a log or a schedule of what they do at home before and after school.

Make a Schedule

Match the clocks that show the same time.
Write something you do at that time of the day or night.

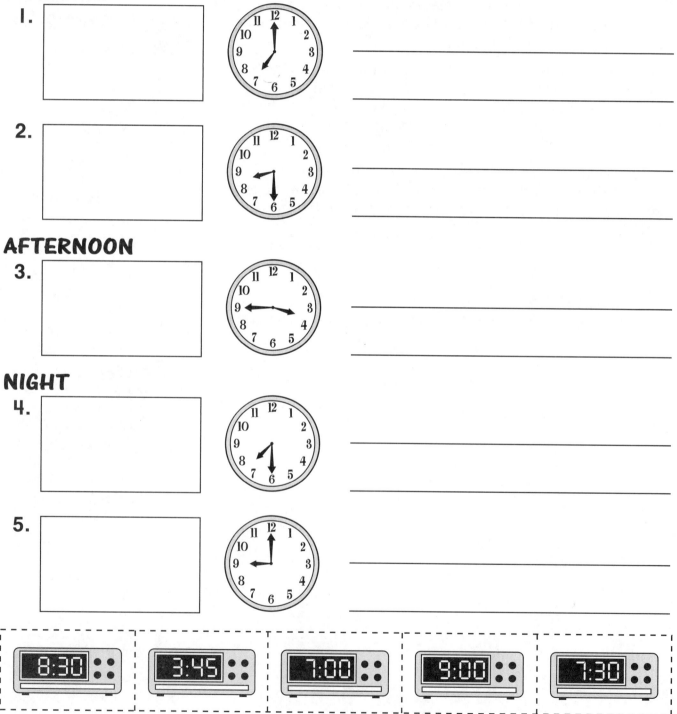

MORNING

1.

2.

AFTERNOON

3.

NIGHT

4.

5.

8:30   3:45   7:00   9:00   7:30

50+ Super-Fun Math Activities: Grade 2 © 2010 by Scholastic Inc.

Just One Minute!

A minute may be longer or shorter than children think as they explore what they can and can't do in just a minute.

PREPARATION

List activities that can and cannot be done in one minute. Suggestions: hop on one foot 30 times; write your name; walk around the room slowly three times; clean out desks or cubbies; count aloud to 100; write the numbers 1 to 100.

DIRECTIONS

1. Write *minute* on the board. Invite children to share what they know about a minute. Demonstrate on a clock with a second hand when a minute begins and when it ends.

2. Present your list of activities that may or may not take one minute to do and ask children to suggest additional activities. Explain to the class that they will be working in groups to find out what they can and can't do in one minute.

3. Select one of the listed activities, or have each group select one. Suggest that children write *yes* or *no* to show whether they think the activity can be done in one minute. Group members can share their ideas before beginning each activity. You may want to be the timekeeper, especially if a large clock is not not available, or have children take turns being timekeeper. The timekeeper tells the group when to begin and when a minute has passed.

4. Be sure children know that this activity is not a race. Have them do each activity without rushing. The point is to know more about what a minute is, not to do these things quickly. At the end of a minute, groups should decide if they could or could not finish the activity. Discuss with children whether their concept of a minute has changed.

ASSESSMENT

Check children's guesses about what they can and can't do in one minute. When children are acting as timekeepers, note whether they know when a minute has passed.

Grouping

Small groups

You'll Need

◆ Clock with a second hand
◆ Pencils

Home Link

Encourage children to guess which of their household routines and activities take more or less than one minute. Suggestions may include brushing their teeth, putting on pajamas, cleaning up after dinner, washing dishes, riding around the block on their bikes, and so on. They might ask a family member to help them time an activity.

Party Time!

Children use events at a party to determine how much time has passed.

DIRECTIONS

1. Talk with children about parties they have attended and the kinds of things they do at parties. Tell them they will be reading a story about a party. They should use what they read to answer questions about the party and to figure out how long the party lasted.

2. You may want to use a demonstration clock to review elapsed time. Move the hands to show 2:00 and then 4:00. Ask how much time has passed. Move the minute hand in 15-minute and half-hour intervals and again have children tell you how much time has passed.

3. Distribute reproducible page 41. Read the story with children. Allow them time to look over the page and ask any questions before they begin.

ASSESSMENT

When children have completed the activity, have them think about questions like these to assess their work:

◆ What did I do to figure out what time different party events happened?

◆ Was it easier to figure out some of the times than others? Why?

◆ What do I still want to know about telling time and how much time has passed?

Answers: 1. 1:00 **2.** 1:30 **3.** 1:45 **4.** 2:15 **5.** 2:30 **6.** 2 hours

➡➡➡ EXTENSION

You might want to have the class run some of the races mentioned in the story and time how long each race takes. (This helps take the emphasis off winning.) They can compare their times to the times in the story.

Party Time!

**Read the story. Draw clock hands to show what
time things happened. Then answer the question.**

> At 1:00 the first guest came. In a few minutes
> everyone was there. At 1:30 we went outside to run
> races.
> We ran three relay races. In the first race, you had
> to keep an egg on your spoon while you ran. That took
> about 15 minutes. The next race was the funniest.
> Each group had a bag of clothes. We had to put on all
> the clothes before we could run. That race lasted a
> half hour. Then we had a skipping relay.
> At 2:30 we had lemonade and watermelon. By 3:00
> the party was over.

1.  first guest comes

2. egg race begins

3. clothes race begins

4. skipping race begins

5. lemonade and watermelon

6. How long did the party last? _____ hours

In This Piggy...

Children follow the clues to find out what coins to put in each piggy bank.

Grouping

Individual

You'll Need

For each child:

◆ **In This Piggy... (reproducible page 43)**

◆ Play money: pennies, nickels, dimes, and quarters

◆ Scissors

◆ Glue or tape

◆ Pencil

Teaching Tip

Suggest that children place their cut-out coins in the banks before they glue or tape them down, to be sure they've used all the coins.

DIRECTIONS

1. Review with children the names of coins and how much each coin is worth. Use pennies, nickels, dimes, and quarters. Say an amount of money and ask volunteers to show the amount with the coins.

2. Tell children they'll now get a chance to be money experts. They'll follow clues to put money in some piggy banks. The trick: there are only enough coins to fill each bank. Distribute reproducible page 43 and review the directions. Be sure that children understand what coin each cut-out stands for. Stress that they'll use all the cut-out coins if they follow the clues carefully.

3. After children have completed the reproducible, have them discuss their work. Was more than one combination of coins possible for any of the clues? Ask children to describe the strategies they used for coming up with the correct amounts.

ASSESSMENT

Ask children to explain why they put each set of coins in each bank. If children make mistakes with the cut-out coins, you might have them model the problems with the play coins. **Answers: 1.** 41 cents **2.** quarter, 3 dimes, 2 nickels **3.** 4 quarters and 1 dime, $1.10.

▶▶▶ EXTENSION

Have children make up new clues for amounts of money in piggy banks. They can exchange sets of clues with partners.

In This Piggy...

Glue the right coins in each bank.

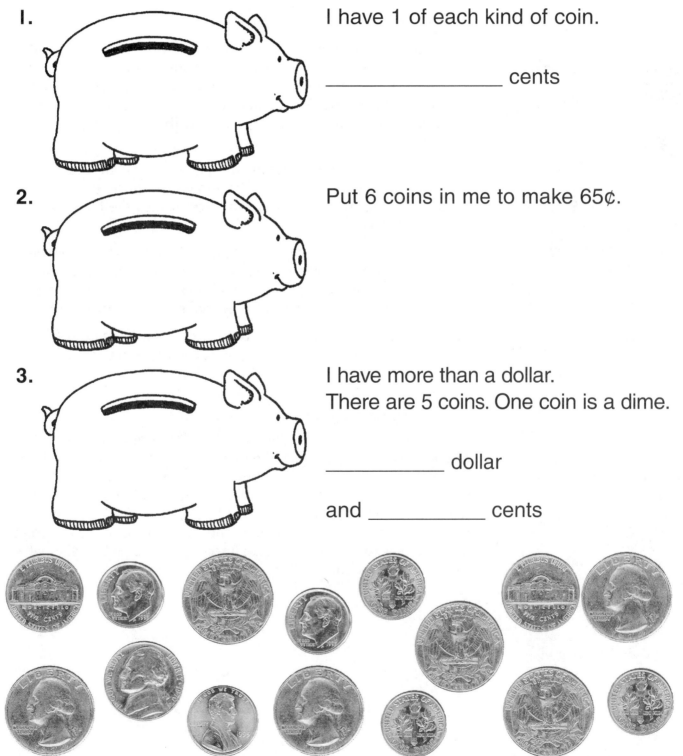

1.

I have 1 of each kind of coin.

_____ cents

2.

Put 6 coins in me to make 65¢.

3.

I have more than a dollar.
There are 5 coins. One coin is a dime.

_____ dollar

and _____ cents

Dollars and Sense

Children discover that number and value are not always equal as they compare amounts of money.

DIRECTIONS

1. Invite children to name the different coins in our money system. Ask them to suggest why we have coins that are different values and why we also have paper money, such as dollar bills. If children have trouble thinking of reasons, ask a volunteer to compare the weight of 200 pennies with the weight of 2 dollar bills. Ask which is easier to carry.

2. Show children three amounts of play money, such as 2 quarters, 5 nickels, and 15 pennies. Ask them which group of coins they would rather have. Point out that sometimes the fewest coins have the greatest value.

3. Distribute reproducible page 45. Explain that children will be choosing from two sets of money each time. Then they will write why they made the choice they did. Have them keep the class's earlier discussion in mind as they make their choices.

4. When everyone is done, encourage children to share their choices. Ask them to identify the set of coins in each pair that is worth more.

ASSESSMENT

You may want to talk with children about their choices and reasons for making them as they work, or when you review their completed pages. Some children may choose a set of coins of lesser value because they like the combination or number of coins, or they would need only that much money to buy something they like. For this reason, it's important to know their reasons for choosing the sets they did. Sets with greater value: **1.** second set **2.** sets are equal **3.** second set **4.** second set **5.** first set

Dollars and Sense

**Look at the two sets of money.
Circle the one you choose.
Then write why you picked it.**

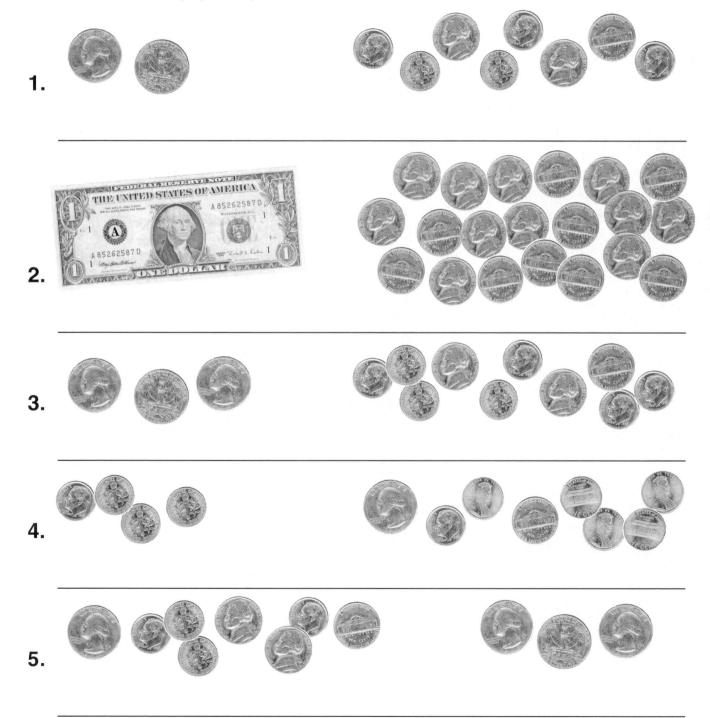

1.

_____

2.

_____

3.

_____

4.

_____

5.

_____

Make-a-Dollar

Children play a game to explore how much money they need to make $1.

Grouping

Pairs

You'll Need

◆ Index cards
◆ Play money: pennies, dimes, nickels, and quarters, for each pair
◆ Paper, one sheet for each child
◆ Pencils

Home Link

Have children share the activity with family members. A family member could display a group of coins less than $1. The child says how much more would make $1.

PREPARATION

Make sets of cards. For each set, cut ten index cards in half; write a money amount between 5¢ and 85¢ on each half.

DIRECTIONS

1. If you start with some money, how much more does it take to make $1? Tell children they'll be figuring this out with a partner. Ask children to choose partners, or divide them into pairs. Distribute a set of cards and play money to each pair.

2. To start, one partner picks a card without showing it. He or she uses coins to model the amount of money shown on the card. The second child must figure out how much more money is needed to make $1.

3. Players take turns. They draw a card, model the amount of money, and have the partner tell how much more it would take to make $1. You may want to have children write both the starting amount and the amount still needed as a record of different combinations that make $1.

4. Children can continue until all cards have been drawn.

 ASSESSMENT

Circulate around the room and ask children what different methods they could use to find out how much more they need to make $1. Encourage them to estimate. As a prompt, ask whether they need 30¢ or more to make $1, or name two amounts and ask which number is closer to what they need.

VARIATION

Have children work together to find all the coin combinations they can for amounts of money listed on the cards.

Far and Away

Children graph an average distance to discover how far the class can toss a ball.

DIRECTIONS

1. Ask children how far they think they can throw a ball. Many of their suggestions may use physical referents, for example, from the door to the back wall. Tell children they'll get a chance to try it and to measure just how far they can throw.

2. Explain the activity. Each child will take two turns to throw the ball as far as possible. After each throw, the child stands in the same spot and holds one end of the yarn. His or her partner stretches the yarn to the spot where the ball landed, then cuts the yarn to show the length of the throw.

3. While they wait for the other pairs to throw the ball, children can compare their own lengths of yarn to see if one of their throws was much farther than, or about the same as, the other.

4. Collect all of the yarn lengths. Then divide the yarn lengths among small groups. Have each group measure their yarn lengths with tape measures, rulers, or yardsticks. Record the measurements in feet or yards.

5. With the class, make a list showing the lengths of the yarn pieces. Then graph the distances, using the data from the list. The graph could show how many children threw a certain distance. Ask questions about the data. What was the farthest distance thrown? What was the shortest? What was the most frequently thrown distance?

VARIATION

Children could throw a few different kinds of balls (Wiffle ball, soft-ball, soccer ball) and compare the distances they were able to throw each ball. Ask them why they think the distances varied.

ASSESSMENT

Observe how groups measure their yarn lengths. Make sure they place one end of the piece of yarn at the end of the ruler, yard-stick, or tape measure.

Grouping

Pairs

You'll Need

◆ Soft ball or beanbag
◆ Skein of yarn or large ball of twine
◆ Scissors
◆ Tape measures, rulers or yardsticks
◆ Paper
◆ Pencils

Teaching Tip

You might want to arrange for a school volunteer to bring small groups of children out-side to complete their throws. To speed up the process, provide more than one ball or beanbag for pairs to throw at the same time.

Sprout-Up Seed Chart

Sprouting plants provide children with a measuring project they can do over time.

Grouping

Small groups

You'll Need

◆ Sprout-Up Seed Chart (reproducible page 49), one for each child

◆ Plastic or foam cups, one for each child

◆ Potting soil

◆ Packets of seeds, a different kind for each group

◆ Newspapers

◆ Rulers

◆ Pencils

Home Link

Some children may be able to keep their sprouts growing at home. Encourage them to continue their recording charts with their families.

PREPARATION
Prepare a large graph that children can use to record and compare the growth rates of different sprouts.

DIRECTIONS

1. Help children form small groups. Tell them they will be doing a planting project to compare how quickly different kinds of seeds grow. Show and discuss the different seeds and the plants pictured on the seed packets.

2. Have children spread newspapers on tables or pushed-together desks before volunteers from each group collect the other materials. Explain that each group will be planting a different kind of seed and keeping records of the plants' growth over time. Distribute the materials and help children plant their seeds.

3. After seeds are planted, have children write their names on their cups and place them in a warm, sunny spot. Set up times when children can check their cups and water their plants.

4. When the seeds begin to sprout, distribute reproducible page 49 to each child. Designate a time each week when children will measure their plant's growth and record it on their own charts and on the large class graph. Children may want to help one another measure: one child can hold the plant gently upright while the other holds the ruler and measures. Tell children to find the closest inch to report.

5. After the project is completed, discuss the results. Ask children which kinds of plants grew more quickly. Have children share their charts.

ASSESSMENT
Check children's charts and the class graph to see how well children measure using small units.

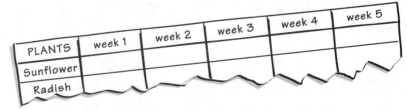

Name_____

Sprout-Up Seed Chart

Kind of seed I planted: _____

WEEK 1	WEEK 2	WEEK 3	WEEK 4	WEEK 5	TOTAL
_____ inches	_____ inches	_____ inches	_____ inches	_____ inches	_____ inches

My Notes

Week 1 _____

_____

Week 2 _____

_____

Week 3 _____

_____

Week 4 _____

_____

Week 5 _____

_____

Munchin' Snack

Children will discover a delicious use for measurement when they make this snack for the class.

Grouping

Small groups

You'll Need

◆ Popped popcorn

◆ Raisins

◆ Chopped nuts

◆ Measuring cups

◆ 3 or 4 large bowls

◆ Large mixing spoons

◆ Paper cups

◆ Napkins

◆ Newspaper

Teaching Tip

Be sure children spread newspaper on the tables. Have groups take turns at a central table for measuring, or distribute ingredients to each group.

PREPARATION

Write the following recipe on large index cards, the chalkboard, or chart paper. Ask volunteers to bring in ingredients. Be sure you have enough of each ingredient for each group to make a batch of Nutty Corn Mix.

> Nutty Corn Mix
>
> 5 cups popped popcorn
> 1½ cups raisins
> 1¼ cups chopped nuts
>
> Mix ingredients together in a large bowl.

DIRECTIONS

1. Invite children to help make a snack for the class. You might want to do this activity on a special day, or invite another class to share the snack.

2. Before beginning the activity, review measuring. Show children a 1-cup measure. Ask them to estimate how many half cups will fill one cup. Call on volunteers to measure the popcorn or another ingredient to check. Do the same with quarter cups. Also have children estimate how many cups will fill a bowl.

3. Have children form three or four small groups. Have them plan how each person in the group will help with the recipe. Encourage groups to find a way for each person to do some of the measuring.

4. After the snack has been made, have groups divide their portions into paper cups so everyone can have some. Discuss the importance of measuring in getting the snack just right.

ASSESSMENT

Observe how children measure each ingredient. Ask how they know they have a cup, a half cup, or a quarter cup.

A Balancing Act

Finding out what weighs a pound may surprise children as they balance a scale.

PREPARATION

Cut off the tops of the milk cartons. Place the pound of clay in one of them. Children will put objects in the other carton.

DIRECTIONS

1. Set out the balance scale and briefly demonstrate how to use it.

2. As you hold up the lump of clay, tell children that it weighs one pound. Invite the class to find out how many crayons, markers, blocks, or other objects equal a pound. Suggest that children first hold the clay to feel its weight. Then have them estimate and record how many of an object they think they will need to balance the weight of the clay.

3. One child places the carton with the clay on one side of the balance scale, while another child puts the empty carton on the other side. They fill the second carton with classroom objects, such as crayons, until the cartons balance. Then, next to their estimate, they record how many crayons equal one pound.

4. Discuss with children how close their estimates were to the actual numbers.

ASSESSMENT

Observe children as they work with the balance. Be sure they understand that when the sides of the scale balance, the objects on both sides weigh the same. Ask children to estimate whether they would need more or fewer paper clips than crayons (for example) to make a pound. Encourage them to explain.

Grouping

Whole class

You'll Need

◆ Balance scale

◆ Lump of clay or other object that weighs one pound

◆ Two empty half-gallon milk cartons

◆ Crayons, pencils, blocks, and other classroom objects available in sufficient quantities to weigh a pound

Home Link

Invite children to find a number of objects at home that they think might weigh a pound. Encourage them to bring the objects to class, with a family member's permission, and use the scale to check their estimates.

Fraction Flags

Making flags will help children develop understanding of equivalent fractions.

PREPARATION

Cut the edge from an 8½- by 11-inch sheet of paper to make an 8½-inch square. Make one for each child.

DIRECTIONS

1. Demonstrate folding a square of paper in half to show children how to match the edges. Open the square and draw a dark line on the fold. Ask children how many equal parts they see. Point out that each part is one half. Explain that the paper can be divided into more equal parts by folding more than once. Tell children they will be folding and coloring papers to make fraction flags.

2. Give each child a paper square. Have them fold the paper one, two, three, or four times.

3. After opening the paper, children can create a pattern by coloring the parts. For example, a paper folded into sixths could be colored with alternating blue and red stripes.

4. Invite children to share their flags with the class. Ask volunteers to tell how many equal parts their flags have, then use a fraction to describe one part.

5. Point out that all of the flags are the same size but that many of them have a different number of equal parts. For example, some flags may be divided in halves, thirds, fourths, sixths, or eighths.

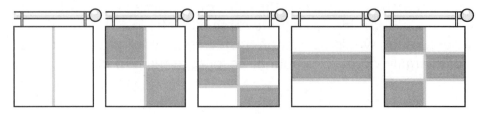

ASSESSMENT

Check that children are folding their papers in equal parts.

Flower Shop Fractions

Children can color a pretty bouquet to help them understand fractions.

DIRECTIONS

1. Have 4 girls and 1 boy stand in front of the room. Review fractional parts of a set by asking children what fraction of the group is girls (four fifths) and boys (one fifth). Remind children that when a fraction represents a group, the bottom number (or denominator) tells the number in the whole group, and the top number (or numerator) tells how many we are talking about. Show children how to write the fractions for the girls in the group ($\frac{4}{5}$) and the boys in the group ($\frac{1}{5}$).

2. Ask children to imagine they work in a flower shop, helping get bunches of flowers ready for delivery. Distribute reproducible page 54 and read the directions with children. Allow time for children to complete the page and then share their work in small groups. Ask questions about the numerator and denominator of each fraction so children relate them to the number in the whole group and the number they colored.

ASSESSMENT

Ask children why they colored the sets of flowers as they did. Have them name the colors in a bouquet and describe what fraction of the flowers are each color. It's not necessary now that children know the terms *numerator* and *denominator*, but they should understand what each part of a fraction represents.

✦✦✦ VARIATION

Have children work in pairs. As one child shows his or her flowers, the other can "order" a bouquet by saying which colors and how many flowers of each color are wanted.

Grouping

Individual

You'll Need

For each child:

◆ **Flower Shop Fractions (reproducible page 54)**

◆ Crayons or markers

◆ Pencil

Flower Shop Fractions

**Choose 2 colors for each bunch of flowers.
Color some of the flowers one color.
Color the rest of the flowers the other color.**

**Write a fraction to tell how many flowers
there are of each color.**

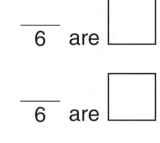

1.

$\dfrac{}{8}$ are ☐

$\dfrac{}{8}$ are ☐

2.

$\dfrac{}{6}$ are ☐

$\dfrac{}{6}$ are ☐

3.

$\dfrac{}{5}$ are ☐

$\dfrac{}{5}$ are ☐

Rock-and-Roll Multiplication

Children roll twice, once for the number of groups to make, and again for the number of objects in each group.

DIRECTIONS

1. Tell children they will be rolling a number cube to find out how many groups of connecting cubes to make, and rolling again to find out how many cubes to put in each group. For example, if a child rolls a 2 and then a 5, he or she makes 2 groups with 5 cubes in each group. When they have made the groups, they can find the total number of cubes and write a multiplication sentence. Demonstrate a few examples with the whole class as a volunteer rolls a number cube. Help children form the habit of recording their number sentences correctly: 3 groups of 6 should be expressed as 3 x 6.

2. Children can take turns rolling the number cube and recording number sentences.

3. Suggest that children record their number sentences in sets according to the number of groups they make. For example, whenever they make three groups, they write those number sentences in one column of a sheet of paper.

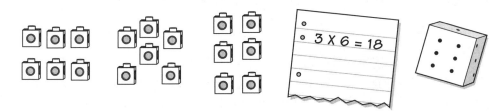

4. Invite groups to share their multiplication sentences with the class.

ASSESSMENT

This is a fairly concrete multiplication activity. Talk with children about what they are doing and what the word *times* means when they use it in a multiplication sentence.

Grouping
Small groups

You'll Need

For each group:
- Number cube labeled 1–6
- 36 connecting cubes or other countables
- Paper
- Pencils

Frame It

Multiples on a hundred frame show multiplication facts.

Grouping

Individual

You'll Need

For each child:

◆ **Hundred frame or reproducible page 29**

◆ Crayons, markers, or colored pencils

Teaching Tip

Coloring lightly will preserve the numbers and make it easier for children to see the number patterns as well as color patterns.

Writing Connection

Ask children to find numbers that are colored more than once. Have them explain why this happens. For example, why does 12 get colored when counting by 2, 3, 4, and 6?

PREPARATION

Make several copies of the hundred frame for each child.

DIRECTIONS

1. Have children look at the hundred frame while you explain the activity. Demonstrate how to use the frame to show counting by 2s. Point out that coloring every second square on the whole chart would show the product of 2 times many numbers.

2. Have children choose another number (4, for example) and color every fourth square on the hundred frame. Encourage children to talk about the patterns that emerge as they continue to color squares on the frame.

3. When children have colored the frame for a given number, show them how to use the filled-in squares to write multiplication sentences beginning with that number multiplied by 1. The colored-in numbers will be the products, or multiples. For example, 1 x 4 = **4**; 2 x 4 = **8**; 3 x 4 = **12**.

ASSESSMENT

As children are working, circulate about the room and ask children questions about the numbers they use to skip count. For example: What is 4 x 6? 3 x 3? Encourage children to use the number patterns they have colored on their hundred frame to help them figure out the answer.

Last-Minute Raisins

Children add last-minute raisins to cookies as they divide, with and without raisins left over.

DIRECTIONS

1. Invite children to imagine that they work in a bakery for a very fussy baker. This baker likes to put exactly the same number of raisins in each giant oatmeal cookie. To make matters worse, the raisin dispenser will give out only 20 raisins at a time!

2. Distribute reproducible page 58 and counters. Explain that children can use the counters to help them figure out how many raisins they can put on the cookies in each group. Remind them that they are to use 20 raisins for each numbered batch. They should put as many raisins as they can on each cookie, but it must be the same number of raisins on each of the cookies in each group. If there are raisins left over, they should record the number in the space provided.

3. When they have raisins divided using their counters, they should draw the raisins on each cookie.

4. Invite children to discuss how many raisins they were able to put on each cookie. Talk about the different strategies children used to figure out how many raisins should go on each cookie.

ASSESSMENT

Encourage children to tell how they figured out the number of leftover raisins for each group of cookies.

 **Grouping**
Individual

 **You'll Need**

For each child:
◆ **Last-Minute Raisins (reproducible page 58)**
◆ 20 counters
◆ Pencil

Last-Minute Raisins

Start with 20 raisins each time. Put the same number of raisins on each cookie.

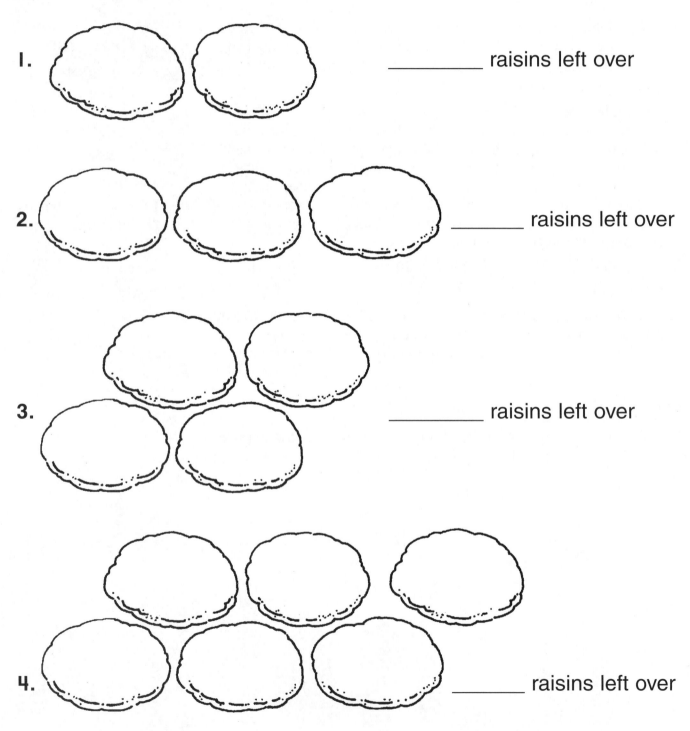

1. _____ raisins left over

2. _____ raisins left over

3. _____ raisins left over

4. _____ raisins left over

Problems and More

Here are more problems you can pose to your class. On the next page is a reproducible with problems children can tackle on their own.

1. SOCK COUNT

Michael helped fold the laundry one day. If he folded 18 pairs of socks, how many socks did he fold in all? Use the quickest way you know to find out.

2. HOW MANY CHAIRS?

Three second-grade classes are going to watch a movie. The first class has 24 children. The second class has 29 children, but 2 are out sick. The third class has 26 children. How many chairs are needed? (Don't forget a teacher in each class.) Draw a picture to help you.

3. NUMBER TWINS

Write some examples of numbers that have the same number of ones and tens. How are the numbers alike?

4. CHECK YOUR ANSWER

How many numbers are greater than 12 and less than 25? Write the numbers.

5. STACK 'EM UP

Len has 12 nickels. If he puts them in stacks of 6, how many stacks will he have? What other ways can Len make equal stacks with 12 nickels?

6. MAKE YOUR OWN!

Give children the information. Ask them to pose problems. See how many different problems children can create with the same facts.

◆ Janell collects 17 stamps. Peter collects 12.

◆ Martha has 20 cookies. Meg has 3 more.

◆ Pilar rode her bike for 10 minutes. Seth rode his bike for 15 minutes.

◆ Adam has 8 toy cars, Jason has 12, and Jean has 9.

Name_____

Problems and More

Put on your thinking cap to solve these problems!

1. GRAPH ADDITION
   How many books did each person read?

   _____

   How many books did they read in all? _____

Books We Read This Year	
Luis	🔲🔲🔲🔲🔲🔲🔲
Julie	🔲🔲🔲🔲
Charles	🔲🔲🔲🔲🔲🔲🔲🔲
🔲 = 5 books	

2. PATTERN PIECES
   There's a number missing in each pattern. Write the missing numbers.

   3, 6, 9, _____, 15   1, 2, 4, 8, _____, 32   1, 2, 3, 5, 8, _____,

   21

3. ONES, TENS, AND HUNDREDS
   Use 2, 7, and 8. Write all the numbers you can make.

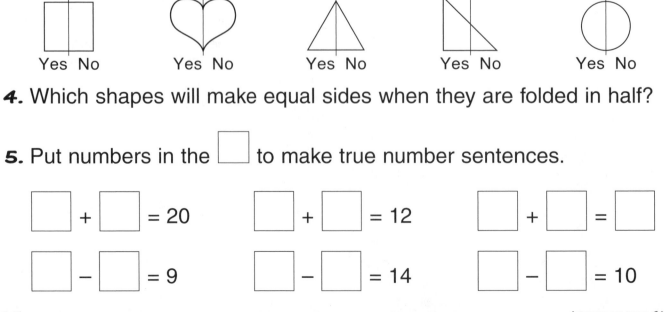

   Yes No   Yes No   Yes No   Yes No   Yes No

4. Which shapes will make equal sides when they are folded in half?

5. Put numbers in the ☐ to make true number sentences.

   ☐ + ☐ = 20   ☐ + ☐ = 12   ☐ + ☐ = ☐

   ☐ – ☐ = 9   ☐ – ☐ = 14   ☐ – ☐ = 10

50+ Super-Fun Math Activities: Grade 2 © 2010 by Scholastic Inc.

Answers on page 64.

An Assessment Toolkit

Alternative methods of assessment provide a comprehensive profile for each child. As children work on their activities in *50+ Super-Fun Math Activities: Grade 2*, here are some ways you might observe and record their work. Alone or in combination, they can provide a quick snapshot that adds to your knowledge of children's development in mathematics. They also give you concrete observations to share with families at reporting time.

FILE CARDS

An alphabetical file system, with a card for each child, provides a handy way to keep notes on children's progress. Choose a few children each day that you plan to observe. Pull their cards, jot down the date and activity, and record comments about their work.

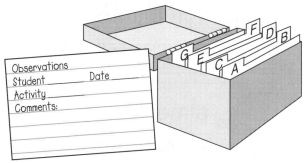

CLIPBOARDS

With a list of children attached to your clipboard, you can easily move about the classroom and jot down observations about their work and their thinking. If you want to focus on a particular skill or competency, you can create a quick checklist and simply check as you observe.

STICKY NOTES

As you circulate while individuals or small groups are working, create a sticky note for children who show particular strengths or areas for your attention and help. Be sure to date the note. The advantage to this technique is that you can move the notes to a record folder to create a profile; you can also cluster children with similar competencies as a reminder for later grouping.

CHECKLISTS AND RUBRICS

On Pages 62 and 63, you'll find a few ready-made checklists and a rubric. Feel free to modify them to suit your own needs. Invite children to assess their own work—they are honest and insightful, and you'll have another perspective on their mathematical development!

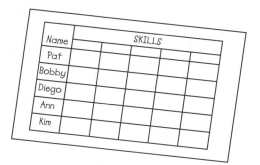

Self-Evaluation Form

ACTIVITY _____

1. I listened to directions…

☐ … almost always
☐ … sometimes
☐ … not very often

2. I followed directions…

☐ … almost always
☐ … sometimes
☐ … not very often

3. I could do the mathematics…

☐ … almost always
☐ … sometimes
☐ … not very often

4. I could explain my work…

☐ … almost always
☐ … sometimes
☐ … not very often

5. I cooperated with my group…

☐ … almost always
☐ … sometimes
☐ … not very often

50+ Super-Fun Math Activities: Grade 2 © 2010 by Scholastic Inc.

Assessment Checklist

Activity _____ Date _____ Group _____

Students					
MATHEMATICS KNOWLEDGE					
Understands problem or task					
Formulates and carries out a plan					
Explains concepts clearly					
Uses models or tools appropriately					
Makes connections to similar problems					
Can create similar problems					
MATHEMATICAL PROCESSES					
Justifies responses logically					
Listens carefully to others and evaluates information					
Reflects on and explains procedures					
LEARNING DISPOSITIONS					
Tackles difficult tasks					
Perseveres					
Shows confidence in own ability					
Collaborates/shares ideas					

SCORING RUBRIC

3 Fully accomplishes the task

Shows full understanding of the central mathematical idea(s)

Communicates thinking clearly using oral explanation or written, symbolic, or visual means

2 Partially accomplishes the task

Shows partial understanding of the central mathematical idea(s)

Written or oral explanation partially communicates thinking, but may be incomplete, misdirected, or not clearly presented

1 Does not accomplish the

Shows little or no grasp central mathematical id

Recorded work or ora explanation is fragm not understandabl

Answers to Problems and More

PAGE 35

1. Jeremy went to bed first, a half an hour earlier.

2. Bill has 80¢. Jessica has 92¢. Jessica has more money. Together they have $1.72.

3. Answers include:
1 quarter, 1 dime, 1 penny
1 quarter, 2 nickels, 1 penny
1 quarter, 1 nickels, 6 pennies
1 quarter, 11 pennies
1 dime, 5 nickels, 1 penny
1 dime, 4 nickels, 6 pennies
1 dime, 3 nickels, 11 pennies
1 dime, 2 nickels, 16 pennies
1 dime, 1 nickel, 21 pennies
1 dime, 26 pennies
2 dimes, 3 nickels, 1 pennies
2 dimes, 2 nickels, 6 pennies
2 dimes, 1 nickel, 11 pennies
2 dimes, 16 pennies
3 dimes, 1 nickel, 1 pennies
3 dimes, 6 pennies
1 nickel, 31 pennies
2 nickels, 26 pennies
3 nickels, 21 pennies
4 nickels, 16 pennies
5 nickels, 11 pennies
6 nickels, 6 pennies
nickels, 1 penny
pennies

vers will vary.

ers will vary.

gave Rodney 6 cookies. Tony had 6
ch child has 4 cookies.

PAGE 36

1. 17 triangles

2. They show the same time in different ways.

3. Children should complete the shapes.

4. Answers will vary.

PAGE 59

1. 36 socks

2. 80 chairs

3. They have the same digit in each place. Examples: 11, 22, 88.

4. 12 numbers: 13, 14, 15, 16, 17, 18, 19, 20, 21, 22, 23, 24

5. 2; 2 stacks of 6, 6 stacks of 2, 3 stacks of 4, 4 stacks of 3, 12 stacks of 1

6. Answers will vary. Children should use the information in their problems.

PAGE 60

1. Luis read 35 books; Julie read 25; Charles read 40. In all they read 100 books.

2. 12; 16; 13

3. 2, 7, 8, 27, 28, 72, 78, 82, 87, 278, 287, 728, 782, 827, 872

4. Yes; Yes; Yes; No; Yes

5. Answers will vary. Check to see that sums and differences are correct.